Wild With It

WILD WITH IT

poems by

Aliki Barnstone

THE SHEEP MEADOW PRESS
RIVERDALE-ON-HUDSON, NEW YORK

All inquiries and permission requests should be addressed to:
The Sheep Meadow Press
PO Box 1345
Riverdale-on-Hudson, NY 10471

Designed and typeset by S.M.
Distributed by The University Press of New England.

Printed on acid-free paper in the United States. This book meets the guidelines for permanence and durability of the Committee on Production Guidelines for Book Longevity of the Council on Library Resources.

The Library of Congress Cataloging-in-Publication Data

Barnstone, Aliki.
  Wild with it : poems / by Aliki Barnstone.
    p. cm.
  ISBN 1-878818-93-7 (pbk. : alk. paper)
  I. Title.

PS3552.A72 W55 2001
811'.54--dc21

                                                        00-067101

This publication is made possible with public funds from the New York State Council on the Arts, a state agency.

The Sheep Meadow Press gratefully acknowledges the National Endowment for the Arts for their support.

ACKNOWLEGMENTS

Grateful acknowledgement is made to the journals in which the following poems have appeared or will appear, sometimes in different form.

Barrow Street: "You Will"

Berkeley Poetry Review: "One Day"

The Blue Moon Review (www.thebluemoon.com): "My Ghost Looks for You," "I Take the Staten Island Ferry to Meet You in the City"

Boulevard: "Months in the Frozen World"

The Drunken Boat (www.thedrunkenboat.com): "In the Basement of the Body," "Childhoods," "Questions on Serifos," "Wild With It," "Wild Wind," "Bedtime Story on Serifos," "Blue," "Bathing Jesus," "Digressions," "Good for You," "Surgery," "Love Asleep," "Walking Around Santa Cruz," "My Career as a Flyer," Euphoria at Zero," "Looking Back with the Angels"

Faultline: "Wild Wind," "Job Interview in North Carolina"

Luna: "Day's of 1974," "Cavafy's Ghost Visits Me at my Mailbox at Bucknell University"

Manoa: "Blue"

Many Mountains Moving: "Resurrection"

New Letters: "The Train to the Millennium," "With Walt Whitman on the Staten Island Ferry," "Wavelength Revelation"

Ploughshares: "You Open Your Hands"

The Southern Review: "Inevitable Move," "The June my Greek Grandmother Lay Dying in a Queen's Hospital"

Southwest Review: "Purple Crocuses"

"Blue" and "Bathing Jesus" appear in *Voices of Light: Spiritual and Visionary Poems by Women Around the World from Ancient Sumeria to Now* (Shambhala Publications, 1999), edited by Aliki Barnstone.

"Bathing Jesus" appears in *Archetypes of the Collective Unconscious: Reflecting American Culture Through Literature and Art*, edited by Mark Waldman (Tarcher / Putnam).

I am grateful for a fellowship from the Pennsylvania State Council on the Arts that helped me complete this book.

Thank you to following friends and family for their encouragement, feedback on poems, and for staying close: Elli, Robert, Tony, and Willis Barnstone, Beth Binhammer, David Birnbaum, Joseph Clark, Lesley Christoph, Kathleen Crown, Debra Gregerman, Tim Fuller, Cynthia Hogue, Dan James, David Kramer, Kathleen Page, Lisa Rhoades, Gerald Stern, and Ruth Stone. Thanks to Kim Addonizio and Margot Schilpp for their incisive comments, which sparked crucial revision, and to Alan Michael Parker for his brilliance and his many hours of attention. Deepest gratitude to Stanley Moss for his belief and his keen editorial advice. Thank you to Zoë for daily lessons in seeing with the eye of wonder.

For my husband, Joseph Clark, and our daughter, Zoë Marika.

CONTENTS

BLUE

Couldn't my love be in that fire, wouldn't she
just adore those ashes, wouldn't she just love to stir

a stick in that dust, and wouldn't she love to dream
of another birth and another conversion?

Couldn't she get on her knees? Couldn't she also
smear her face with dirt? Couldn't she explode?

Gerald Stern

BLUE

She must have been there
the morning my daughter was born,
blue in the windows;

the narrow glass in the hospital walls
let in her pale spring light.
She hides in the forget-me-nots in the wallpaper,

flutters in the doctors' and nurses' dull medical gowns,
glints in the metal of the scissors that cut the cord.
Her threads embroider the bloody placenta.

She tints the newborns' eyes with her cyan hand,
for babies come from her inside-out world.
She is in the spit against the evil eye.

When I'm blue I close my eyes and see her light
coming from the Greek island in my brain
where sunflowers crook their necks, weary of time,

their wild hair burning in the sky of her wide mind.
I float naked in her color, the sea
hums in my ears, lulling me

like a baby kicking in amniotic waters.
Her throne is a transparent bowl,
a star-sapphire studded cradle of waves.

She must make love on silk sheets of air.
She must have blue skin and eyes,
her breasts amply squirting milk,

lapis lazuli looped in strands and strands
around her arms and her rounded belly.
Peaceful blue, luminous blue, keep my daughter safe.

See, she splashes her little feet in the Aegean,
reaches her hands into sky. I hug her dry
in a towel deep blue as Mary's timeless robes.

THE JUNE MY GREEK GRANDMOTHER
LAY DYING IN A QUEENS HOSPITAL

my brothers, our lovers, and I sat on the terrace on Serifos,
calling out to the owls, calling out *Who? Who? Who?*

pushing out the air and O of mystery from our throats,
then swallowing potent island wine, slightly sweet

and complex, while the owls called back
from their rocky home, intimate yet distant,

and taught their young to fly from cliff to cliff.
The full moon rose from the mountain's knobby knees,

rocky breasts, sleeping shoulders, and I called to the owls,
a mourning cry, a shriek or moan, a supplication

all the way to Queens—*Yiayia, live!*
though I knew *she* prayed for a quick end.

Occasionally an owl might perch on a wire above us,
keeping its body still, except the quizzical watching head.

I remember her bent head as she read or sewed,
her round owl torso, her beak of a nose,

her canny eyes, her kiss as she blessed me
with the sign of the cross and said, *my child.*

Now the moon turns our whitewashed walls to glass,
turns the night sea to milk and sends its shimmer

far across the water to light distant islands. This is the warm sea
she loved, where I floated in her arms when I was small,

hypnotized by light writing the dazzled alphabet on water.
Silently an owl alights on our open windowsill.

My husband takes my hand as she looks at us
and our baby sleeping between us. How large she is,

her silhouette against the moon, watching our family
steadfastly and so long I fall asleep with her still there.

She flies away unbeknown to me.
The white heat of the Greek sun wakes her gone.

MY CAREER AS A FLYER

My workshop smells of wax and ash and flesh. You can see,
    I've made my shoulderblades into feathered muscles.
Now flapping my arms, tricks shimmering on my lips like silver coins,
    angling between the shades of skyscrapers,
I'm wowed by a perfect accident: a jet flies across the full moon.
    Finding you will be like that good omen
or the dart pitched in absolute darkness, striking the bull's eye.
    Friends dance on a checkerboard floor,
and there I am, happy among the group,
    music laying firm hands on my body,
in this room yet sidling up the fire escape, taking off
    over rooftops and palms, into the panorama
of light-studded hills and freeways,
    the thousands of shadowed minds surging
white, red, white, red headlights onto and off the Bay Bridge.
    I soar into the euphoria of the wino in the Tenderloin,
who calls out, "Hey, girl! Take me home and save me!"
    If someone says, "Why don't you take a flying fuck?"
I think, Why not? Why not a flying, wet, wingéd fuck,
    our bodies iridescent among the clouds, solid life
rocking the color plane like Franz Marc's blue and red horses,
    like fleshy trees arching into each other,
dancing mud or sheets and sheets of orange silk
    flowing from the sun floating in your blue eye.
See how my body rises, the sea's pigment rising with me
    to stain my skin, and I glide blue, spiraling above
freighters and tugboats and bridges of the Bay.
    The towers wink out red warnings:
you can't help where you go, can't help flying out of yourself.
    Look up, you can see me above the city,
the wind in my mouth, the night ink on my hands.

CHILDHOODS

1.
Outside the car windows dogwood are a thousand
white flashes in the woods. New green
recedes into the circular red barn and the neat farmhouse
where oak trees line a gravel lane and two black carriages
rest in the lot. No electric or telephone wires lead there.
The Amish farmer drives six horses down the highway,
and fishermen stand up to their crotches in cold water,
casting their lines through mist into the brook.

I'm the strange one here, remembering a dream or something
far away that comes and goes like these scenes sucked away
through windows.

       Some child climbs out of the water and running
toward me with hands out for these blackberries,
so sweet I scarcely put half in the colander for pie and jam,
and stain my white pants, big hand prints down my thighs.
What's your name? I say.
       You name me, says the child, you name me.

What a lulling voice you have when I fall into the manhole,
not minding at all because I float down like Alice, my other name,
then always float back up again elsewhere,
       say, on a Santa Cruz bus.
Outside are seals, cormorants and pelicans, surfers and cyclists,
monarch butterflies drifting in air sharp with ocean and eucalyptus.

The bus exhales as it pulls into the next stop.

       Who is it?
The girl standing before me, her fingertips on the rail, just the tips—

she doesn't need to hold it—bends her knees a little with the lurches,
and balances there with one sock up, one sock down, one button
of her jacket buttoned, one fist in a pocket, strands of hair freeing
themselves from her braid, and she stares, just like me.
How can she be?
    How can I fall back into sleep, letting my breath out
slow, slow, slipping under the surface, belly first, where shining
pebbles shift with urchins and coin-sized abalones.
        How can I
let her disappear again so I can stumble-leap down bus stairs,
calling out *thank you!* to the silent driver. He won't tell the route,
won't tell the street names, but the houses are familiar
and the gardens full of flowers whose names I can recite:
lobelia, delphinium, camellia.
      When I call out *hi!* to the clean-cut guy
with weeds in one hand, garbage in the other, she'll find me again,
her hair wild, dripping with fever and weeping.
      Though she is
nonbeing, and I wake to find her and wake to find her and wake
to find her gone again, she'll ask why I chose to send her away,
why I let her and her brother flash their life-lights in my window,
only to speed away in one moon cycle, to be sucked away
in a few breaths, one long suppressed scream, my fleshy being
contracting around nothing, nothing at all, while a machine pumped.

2.
Now in the car, your hand on my thigh, these scenes flicker by
while my voice and your voice admire dogwood and farms,
dark cows below the sunset, clouds a sleek spaceship,
the gingerbread on that sky blue house, the one on the hill.
Let's go home, you say.
    Let's have a cup of tea, I say.
We stand in the kitchen and the steam howls.

I find you through telephone lines, traveling toward me
in cars or books or with a look through the spaces in rooms.
We coil and turn, your hand on the small of my back,
your chest against mine, breath on breath, legs intertwining.
I see my eyes in yours, as we call out, come, laugh.
You put your hand on my abdomen. There were two.
Who are they? The boy with berry-stained lips and hands,
the girl with her falling sock and staring brown eyes.

                                               They are
these words on the screen, on the page, on the round air in our mouths
before we speak, or perhaps they are old snapshots thumbtacked
to the wall, you or me, your blond hair, cheekbones,
the grave humor in your voice, your fine-boned hands, my skinny calves,
belly sticking out, my dark eyes and too-sensitive nose,
no attribute, no word makes sense of these children
whom I will never hold, nor will I stop traveling back
to where they are not, not even when I give birth.

IN THE BASEMENT OF THE BODY

We hold each other in the basement of the body.
Through the high windows nine full moons shine.

Who will you be when we are three?
Will you be my wild lover?
Will you travel by my side, steadfast?

The skin of your belly warms the skin of my belly,
and our baby climbs like a mountain goat
quick against my ribs.

Yet there is distance to traverse.

Outside these walls in a wild field poppies are blood,
crickets and birds
and new frogs the size of pennies
leap and sing from the grasses.

At the horizon the forest is a dark feather.

Before I return home to you with our child—
through unlit woods, all the way across the field—
I must labor with this quivering weight.

FACE CELLS

Babies have "face cells" in their brains, whose purpose is to recognize their mothers' facial features.

You come into the world seeing
only as far as my breast and face

for your life depends on knowing me
and there are cells in your baby brain

just for recognizing—
out of the chaos

of shadow and light—my face.
You scan me, shape me,

memorize the feathered sweep of hairline,
almond curve of eyelids,

movement of irises
looking back,

a flesh moon
rising in the room's outer space

(lips—dark, plump—
kiss, smile, coo).

You see me see you,
make me as I made you.

RAINY GHAZAL

I watch drops gather on the windowpane,
swelling up, trembling with their weight,

then shuffle off, silver elephants and snakes.
I make cities in the glass—narrow streets, a maze

of slicked stone and neon signs, a blaze
of stars radiating from water, a galaxy of rain.

Around me other girls and boys, the lesson of restraint.
Above our heads, chugging the walls, is a train,

cardboard placards of the alphabet, big *A*,
little *a*, big *B*, little *b*, each letter a face,

a character acting on the page like rain
scribbling itself on glass. Each drop has a name.

Other children tell me not to stare. Teacher explains.
They talk and language pools, pocked with rain,

and won't be a mirror. Rain, rain go away.
No, come back. I'd like to play. Fight away the shame

of being by trying to see the shape
between us, the ghost of air, the space

between the drops. What does the rain say?
Rain. Rain down rain down rain down rain down. Rain.

Your ear's on the desk, Aliki. Let your brain
rest. Let your pencil write a watery refrain.

JOB INTERVIEW IN NORTH CAROLINA

Rain on the sound, rain on the hotel window,
on the highway slick and reflecting dark palms
breathing the wind.

Yesterday I was welcomed and imagined myself
here, the sun a balm on my skin.

Rain on the sailboats moored in rows in sand,
rain on ducks hunched on the shore.

And they bragged about the beauty, pointed
to the long leaf pines, their luxurious needles
of light shifting in the breeze.

Rain on the parking lot blacktop, an ink wash
thinning into gray water,
spiked by wharves, blotted by marshes.

The ocean churned out mist
and pelicans glided through corridors of waves.
I stood here already seduced, he said,
as there I stood already seduced.

Rain tapping out the rhythm of the nursery rhyme
I chant to my daughter.
Rain on the green grass, rain on the tree,
rain on the rooftop but not on me.
As if I could be impervious to judgment.

An egret stood still as a new moon in the wetlands
and I wanted them to want me.

Rain on the man unfurling his umbrella, a black poppy.

I touched pansies blooming in January.

He moves toward shelter, head bent
as if there were something to mourn.

CAVAFY'S GHOST VISITS ME AT MY MAILBOX
AT BUCKNELL UNIVERSITY

don't futilely mourn your luck giving out, your work
collapsing, the designs of your life
that have all proved to be illusions.
                              C.P. Cavafy

Professor Barnstone's petty disappointments
lie inside this box.

And you, Cavafy, stand at the end of the hall,
your glasses glinting in the humid light
of the summer-empty building.

Your ghostly body still feels secret pleasures,
the jasmine skin you touched
above the suspect taverna,
the ugly, dirty room,

the narrow window with its narrow view
of the alley, the garbage
leaning against the buildings as if resigned;
outside the kitchen window

newly washed plates and glasses drying on a shelf,
the odors of olive oil, smoke, and coffee
mixing with the boy's delicate, erotic sweat.

You worked as a clerk for the Irrigation Service by morning,
walked home afternoons with the sea-salt burning
your nostrils, the sun heating your back, Eros

and the music of poetry fervid inside you.
Printing your poems in secret, only for the select,
you didn't let Alexandria have you.

I want you to speak
but all your words are memory—
the letter you wrote—

how this place disturbs me.
What trouble, what a burden small cities are—
What lack of freedom—

In 1925 when Mildred Martin came here to teach,
the villagers told her it was a scandal
for her to shut her blinds at night.
All should see that she concealed

nothing in the electric light's unflattering yellow—
as if the gesture of covering shame
were proof of the act.

Cavafy, you would esteem the students,
the intelligence on their young skin.
And you too would be despised
for what it does no good to try to hide.

I'd like to take your arm and walk below
the maple trees whose leaves are a jumble
of words that come together then shift apart—

obstacle, walls, burned out candles, the god
who abandons me.

I'd like to hear your breath beside me
as I walk this small city,
past these windows, these framed tyrannies—

you'd hear the whispers issuing from artificial light,
even as I mutter my true name.

PURPLE CROCUSES

Seduced by El Niño's eastern balm, they bloom early.
One morning they appear, sudden like shining wet paint
splashed across the newly green lawn.

They've naturalized, their opulent purples
each year more abundant with drunken bees
buzzing between six pointed petals.

Purple crocuses with shocking orange centers
were here before I stuck my shovel in this dirt,
perhaps before the old widow, Elvira Lockwood,

who dug here before me and left a wind chime
for her ghost to breathe against
while the red-throated house finches warble,

who, a neighbor woman told me, loved birds and flowers
and planted the climbing rose of pale pink and milk
that never bloomed for us until our daughter's birth.

Even as the hands touch wood, say this house is mine—
the barn, the fence, the rose trellis my love built
for the warm-petalled Joseph's coat to climb,

the dirt under my feet—these purple crocuses
spread under the fence to share themselves with neighbors,
unownable fleeting musical notes for the eye to hear.

YOU OPEN YOUR HANDS

You learned the intimate—
to recognize faces,
latch onto the breast,
cry out your pain,
smile into a smile

—and you held that knowledge close
in your strong reflexive grasp,
as if under your fingers,
those tender miniatures,
a secret lay at the center of your palm.

Now you unfist your hands
and reach into vast air,
pat flowers on the pillowcase,
fan your fingers across my breast,
find you can touch as well as be touched.

As when we two were one,
your body still nestles in mine—
(belly skin meets belly skin, eye meets eye).
Soon your fingers will pull the world
in close to taste, to see

—for you demand I turn you outward
to encounter constellations of faces,
bright slabs of window light.
Oh, small child,
all that patterns and shines mesmerizes you

and you open your hands!
I see how beautifully,

with shudders of excitement,
you enter the open cosmos—
and, in nearly invisible increments,

part from our close circle—

INEVITABLE MOVE

When I take my daughter to the Mennonite woman
who cares for her on afternoons, we pass
the old brick Groves mill, winter cornfields,

neat Pennsylvania Dutch farms, red barns
with solid stone foundations and long white louvers,
painted signs next to the mailboxes proclaiming faith:

on the way there, *Let us draw nigh unto the Lord,*
and *All things were created by God;* on the way home,
Come follow Jesus Christ and *I owe the Lord a morning song.*

The road curves like a dreamy explorer around hills,
under amicable sycamores huddled together, abreast the river,
then over it on two bridges, one steel, one stone.

In the back Zoë babbles at what she sees
through the rear windshield: treetops reach fingertips
toward the colorless sun, tin roofs glint with winter austerity.

Look, Zoë! I call, See three fat geese in the yard!
See the cows! See so many crows in the corn!
(I can't help thinking of Van Gogh's cornfield.

All this beauty will be buried soon in the dirt
of my memory, most of it for good, and Zoë will see it
not at all or in that distant home of dreaming and learning

where a door might be ajar, letting in a slit of light
but no shapes, nothing with a name.)
I wish I could stand barefoot in spring mud

and mortar stone after stone in a wall forever
and plant a Rose-of-Sharon with faith, and never leave.
If I could be like these farmers with their old brick houses,

their history and their mission, I would sing
the Lord a morning song and bless all creation
and stretch my hands toward the supernatural face.

No such luck. I kiss my baby bye bye,
be back soon. Sue holds out her hands
long-fingered and brown, smiles a lovely gap-tooth smile.

My girl flails in gentle arms and wails out her loss
as I drive away, sending up hundreds of crows,
black angels protesting over the implacable landscape.

THE TRAIN TO THE MILLENNIUM

And I saw a new sky and a new earth,
for the first sky and the first earth were gone
and the sea was no more. I saw the holy
city, the new Yerushalayim, coming down
out of the sky from God who prepared her
like a bride adorned for her groom. And then
I heard a great voice from the throne, saying
"Look, now the tent of God is with the people,
and he will spread his tent over them,
and he God himself will be with them,
and he will wipe away each tear from their eyes
and death will be no more. And grief and crying
and pain will be no more. The past has perished."

The Apocalypse
(The Revelation of Saint John)

MONTHS IN THE FROZEN WORLD

for Gerald Stern

In gorgeous, inhospitable snow, crows flap over destitute yards,
their calls tricking back the song the house made when I climbed
upstairs, as if their wings climbed the sky, as if they'd wakened
shades in the underworld, that frozen air. House music.
I'm afraid I'll say it, house music, and break the ice
when I open my savings account. I'm afraid I'll sing
to the nice teller patiently explaining how it works.
I might tell her I feel flush or ambivalent outside the public library

where ghostly books fall down the return tunnel, down there
where I stand in kitchen memory, stirring soup in a big black pot.
I might tell her my blank recollection without regret, a different house.
Grief seizes inside me. I have no choice and look out.
Do I look at the landscape and see myself? I see sun
is snow and fire on the walnut tree whose massive arms form
a comfortless circle where—shouldering air, muscular, comic, hungry—
circumspect crows span their zone with gazes and caws.

The crows. The snow. The lost house. The dream of fire.
I might tell her these months in the frozen world I dream
of fire burning all the money in the bank, lush green-blue flames.
And the bank burns, too, the house, the town, the world,
the newspapers and TVs that tell the tale of charred bills
orbiting like a billion crows over the cinders and the dead.
I might tell her of my slow free-fall toward distant ground,
that the sky blooms with twelve full moons bright

as desert sand. Blue before dawn, blue at twilight,
mournful blue, moonfull sky, the spectacle, time passing.
These are months in the frozen world.
These are things winging into nothing. See how I spiral down

leisurely like a leaf, a feather, like ashes, ashes,
like a crow laughing, you can't die if you invent your death.
I'm so happy as I plunge, telling my joke to the air—
I could spill it all to the woman asking me to sign here.

EUPHORIA AT ZERO

Euphoria is a cobalt winter sky that stings you.
A pink Cadillac fishtails 360 degrees—
then drives on. No accident.
The air deafens your skin, loud with zero and wind.
Cold is a lemon on your tongue. Bittersweet hunger.
You walk over your weaknesses
as if they were a sheet of ice,
knowing their dangers, not minding much,
confident in your big black boots.

DAYS OF 1974

As bright Athenian light glanced off the stunning bodies
of the gods, tall glass cases of ceramics,
and vast marble floors,

he furtively told the two American girls
he met in the Archeological Museum
he was writing an underground guide to the erotic antiquities.

One girl was suspicious and intrigued,
the other liked to talk yet gazed in silence at ancient vases
where the dance of sex unveiled the human divine,

perfect men and women athletically copulating
in twos or threes or even fives,
beaming calm and spiritual smiles.

He was a small man, his hair a little long, an intellectual
with nervous arms, poetic eyes, and shabby clothes.
In America shabby was fashionable, but not in Greece,

not in '74 under the colonels when so much was illegal:
old men playing gin rummy in the cafés and talking politics;
throwing plates to the floor to applaud the dancers' passion.

All names but the Christian ones were banned—
Socrates, Aristotle, Athena, Euridice, Aliki.
Those were the days before the tourist trade took off,

so the museum was empty, except the three of them
and bored guards who thought the young man
a fool who wouldn't get far with the American girls.

The girls couldn't tell—was he a hippie? Did he want them?
(Later one would wonder if he liked girls that way.)
In the museum's celebrating light, he spoke of history and myth

and they trusted him and agreed to meet for a parade
honoring Venezelos, a hero in the conflict
between the Greeks and Turks.

The people lined the street in the April sun,
waved small blue and white Greek flags.
They were dreaming the colors of old embroidery,

gold bangles across a girl's forehead,
the weight of tightly-woven fabric.
They were dreaming of the dance,

the smile running though muscular legs
that trace a maze of steps on pavement
and leap free within form.

A few palace guards marched by in white kilts and leggings,
and then the army and the navy in drab uniforms.
War planes screeched above

while the dreadful tanks climbed the boulevard,
shaking balconies, windows, sidewalks,
the teeth in each skull. No one cheered.

The junta would fall that summer, but today
the young man stood with the two American girls,
thinking what he might whisper as they walked home

past closed shops, tavernas, bakeries, cafés, and smells
of bread and grilling meat, where three old men
sat, legs apart, at sidewalk table, watching the girls go by.

Only a few months ago, the tanks shuddered the same street
and crushed the gates of the *Polytechneo*, where the students
draped banners painted *Eleftheria*, freedom,

and draped themselves, arm in arm, intertwined
like figures on an ancient vase,
until tanks ground hundreds of young bodies under their treads.

He would speak clearly, softly so only they would hear,
and he rehearsed his words, and he watched the girls
watch the grim purposefully silent faces of the crowd.

WAVELENGTH REVELATION

I'm rowing in my small boat on electronic seas,

rowing, rowing in my glass bottomed boat.
The fish swim among holograms of celebrities
and I plunge in to join them in the ocean of news

and oldies, classical, top ten, talk and static,
and drown in radio waves.

The enormous head of consciousness looms like Buddha

over mountains of landfill rising from the shore,
microchips, television litter, radio glitter—

and the beach is tiny glass balls,
bottles, screens, test tubes shattered and worn by the sea.

Sea gulls squawk and dive in sync
with the whirling resistors sensing heat and sound.

My boat bobs in phosphorescence

and I reach for a Milky Way of flashing lights,
the control panel of the universe.

I'm rowing in my small boat on plumbless, hissing seas—

Oh, the electric weave of light, the floating seductive helixes,
the symphony of beeps and squeals, whizzes, buzzing and chirps.

Ah, the winging and winging on synthetic wind—

I'm rowing, rowing toward every horizon,
toward the edges of the screen—

Where are the palm trees? Where the dolphins?
There in that filmy glow out of which everything grows.

RESURRECTION

I took my body with me
and waved goodbye to the angels in my tomb
who sat where my head and feet had been.
I am everywhere alive, a word,
my blood the happy red tulips,
my eyes new leaves blinking in the sun.
I am flesh among you and I am lonely
walking the yellow highway lines,
carrying four brown paper bags
full of newspapers, the sins of the world,
my hair lighted, a halo of mercury
in a candelabra of streetlights.
I leave my footprints to shine, oil on asphalt.
I have a body so I dream of Mary
washing my feet with her tears
and drying them with her hair.
I smell myrrh, remember her anointing fingers,
my cock rising toward paradise.
I am everywhere and I am inside her,
lost in balms, my eyes blazing
as my skin becomes hers,
and I am she,
a woman, flesh and blood, blessing the union.

WITH WALT WHITMAN ON THE STATEN ISLAND FERRY

What is more subtle than this which ties me to the man
  or woman that looks in my face?
Which fuses me into you now, and pours my meaning
  into you?

I sat at ease with Walt on the ferry,
and let my knee lean against his thigh.

An expert in corn flakes, he slipped his hand between wax paper leaves,
infused the cock on the box with iridescence,

found a true word for every crunch,
and blew the words in kisses onto the lips of the crowd.

I guided his hand under my skirt
which was scripted with the looping calligraphy of the city.

He kindly fingered my crack with one hand,
unbuttoned the brown wool of his trousers with the other.

And as I arched to meet him,
he hooked his head on my shoulder, breathing in my ear,

"Jesus Kennedy—Jack Christ—
your social memory began in 1963,

with equal parts dread and ecstasy,"
and I saw my boot on the sidewalk, the bright hopscotch chalk,

the November leaves blown against the fence,
heard the kids calling out, "The President's dead!"

Walt and I knelt on a bed of newspapers,
moaning the holy names, shuddering with the ferry engine,

as the Statue of Liberty, Ellis Island, and the Jersey skyline
floated by with mercury-lighted clouds.

And when it was over, he eyed the grapefruit mounds
of young men's asses, hoisted his bag of books,

and melded into the crowd, into Manhattan.
I followed, staring hard into the place

where Walt Whitman had been,
where yellow flashes of taxis curved by Battery Park

and the lighted windows of skyscrapers stretched
disembodied into the heavenless night.

BATHING JESUS

If he were a word made flesh I would want to wake him from his godliness
and wash his godliness from him as I bathe his feet in my laughing tears
and dry them with my heat and hair and anoint the topography of his head
      with euphoric oil
and comb his beard with electric fingers and pull his face close to mine
to see the multitudes in the pores in his skin, God's intricate human
      handiwork in his cheek.
Jesus would see the flame in my eye burning in time's skull, deep as the first
      breath that lighted the Milky Way.
I would pull the shirt from his shoulders and the shirt from mine
until our garments lay on the floor, cloth lungs pulsing
      with the curtain's white muslin and the little breezes
      coming in the window, everything alive,
even the wood floor under our feet warm with the oak's broad and
      branching spirit.
I would pour warm water on his back and thighs and wake the man in him,
wake his hand reaching for my flushed and water-slicked arm, his palm
      singeing the place below my collarbone,
make him taste each word on my tongue, each complex mix of sweet
      and bitter and sour and salt
and make him sing out from his body, *the lips, the tongue, the throat,*
      the heart, the blood, all the traveling heats of flesh. Praise them.

THE TRAIN TO THE MILLENNIUM

I got an uptown train to the end of the twentieth century.
All my lovers were there, grim as hell, hair spiked with fire,

sexier than sex. I wanted to feel their life-blood strain forward
in the palm of my hand, dig shiny black high-heels into their asses

and make them scream. All my friends were laughing,
our reflections floating in the windows—over brick tenements,

warehouses, garbage, sad smashed cars in junkyards, slag-heaps,
the mowed lawns and token trees of tract homes.

I wanted to love them with my tongue as I never had before.
All the children I never had, all their friends, all my friends' children

ran down the aisles and climbed over the seats, calling out new words,
sweet and cool as apple juice slipping down my throat.

All my family, all my teachers rode with me to the end of the line,
to the enormous station where the tracks stopped,

where windows rose five stories and opened
to a field uninterrupted by the human, to the big peachy afternoon sun,

the new moon above like an ironic smile.
All our dogs were there among the cone flowers and cosmos,

retrieving calendars and dropping them at our feet.
All my students were stoned, milling about, taking in the fractured

station window light, not demonstrating, looking just like those who did.
All the TVs were stacked against a wall, turned on and tuned in

to different channels, entrancing our retinas with the past:
"Beavis and Butthead," "Bewitched," warclips, a boot to a head.

All the typewriters and computers, the obsolete and state of the art,
hung out against the opposite wall, ready to light up, bring on

the next sentence. "Fuck the world!" I called out,
like the crazies on the street below my apartment in San Francisco,

"It's over! The end!" Then I thought, it's the middle not the end,
just another day, and all my friends became strangers carrying briefcases,

women in long coats and white tennis shoes,
kids feeling their bodies under black leather.

"Goodbye," I said to no one. "Goodbye," I said
to the trains moving away on infinite tracks,

heavy with their own weight of steel, their load of people,
newspapers, umbrellas, sandwiches, memory.

WILD WITH IT

SEIZURE

To me he seems like a god
the man who sits facing you
and hears you near as you speak
and softly laugh

in a sweet echo that jolts
the heart in my ribs. For now
as I look at you my voice
is empty and

can say nothing as my tongue
cracks and slender fire is quick
under my skin. My eyes are dead
to light, my ears

pound, and sweat pours over me.
I convulse, greener than grass,
and my mind slips as I
go close to death,

yet I must suffer all things
being poor

                    Sappho

STAGE

The sign says STAGE as if to name the summer street
on which Saturday night revelers trip out of bars,
call out, bump against each other, and laugh too loud
as they step over white line markers
into newly washed and gassed-up trucks.

Stage as if to frame this pain which will fade
into the ink of memory's script
like these lightly dressed people who make appearances
then disappear into the wings like the drunk's tires
screeching above the stereo bass and raging muffler,

then leave the night quiet encompassing

the closed department store called STAGE
and the mind divided, sorting its hidden merchandise
into compartments—passion in a flame dress,
caress of silk falling away, sweaty shirt, sad socks,
shoes of betrayal, a cruel wide belt,
perfumes called hope, devotion, obsession, and misery.

YOU WILL

You will be jealous and hear nothing but jealous, jealous.
You will throw yourself at your lover's feet and beg.
You will pray to Jesus though you don't believe he's God's son.
You will neither eat nor sleep. Your teeth will chatter
and you will rub together chilled hands in ninety degree heat.
You will have the runs as your body tries to shit out the toxin of betrayal.
You will flee home, feeling you have none.
Pain will blind you and you will crash your car.
You will get back on the road and a car will pass you
with vanity plates reading HURT 1.
You will will your will and it will help briefly and briefly again.
You will spin the wheel of karma and count your burdens.
You will hold your baby and weep and bless life.
You will curse the flat landscape, the walls of August corn,
praise the hills climbing from the Mississippi.
You will become small. You will become large.
You will be afraid to speak but rage will speak you.
You will disappear. You will will yourself become will-less.
Your love will speak you. You will speak you.
You will open your mouth and grow many arms and legs.
You will make love, come, call out, cry, each spiraling inside each,
a tango of hair and limbs and rage and tenderness.
You will hear all your lover's music, the high chimes of the soul,
the rhyme of the low animal moan.

WILD WITH IT

You will hardly know who I am or what I mean,
But I shall be good health to you nevertheless,
And filter and fibre your blood.
                    Walt Whitman

I am your underground river, flowing in the dark
beneath the earth's skin, and I am your blood.

I am the Mississippi, lighted and calm,
and the grassy hills clambering from its waters,

and I am your Mississippi flooding its banks, a volcano
flaming the sky to ash, a tidal wave. Because of you,

I am a Greek island redolent with oregano and thyme,
dry salt air. I am the sea voluptuous against your naked thighs,

the sunlight drying the blond hairs on your legs and arms.
I am your sun burning away all sight except its own light,

a sun throbbing, giving the land color and shape,
the little whitewashed house, the bed below the window full

of mountains breathing deep into the earth, bones of knees,
elbows, flesh of breasts and cocks, cunts and shoulders,

broad chest where the heart beats and makes the capers
and daisies tremble, all the nerves, thistles and sticks,

electric and telephone wires buzzing on your flesh.
I am the moonlight showing you how the sea's body stretches

all the way to New York, to streets whitened by oil and rain,
to shoes scuffing the sidewalks, and windows bright

with pots and pans dangling from the ceiling,
lovers and families, bathrooms—a guy's bent head

as he fills the bowl—I am pens, notebooks, computer screens,
I am your world wide web, I am your easy chair—

you hold a book on your knee—mine is the bare belly
appearing before the shade goes down and mine is

the kiss deepening to a bite on your neck.
I am your witch poking pins into a voodoo doll.

She who comes between us I will burn, bury, break,
shoot off in a rocket to the nothing of space.

I am I am I am. And in you I am, for you erase
and make new our two conjugating shapes.

MY GHOST LOOKS FOR YOU

My ghost hangs out on the sidewalk in Wilmington
where the boulevard leads from the highway to your old neighborhood.
She's shuffling past the station where we gassed up our cars
to see each other.
Her shirt is inside out and her socks don't match.
She's smeared a paste of kisses and come and tears
on her face and hair.
She's painted her lips and lined her eyes with the ink of your pen.
My black bra crowns her head.
She muddies her shoes on the banks of the Brandywine river,
feeds Canada geese the bread of her body,
drunk on the wine of your love.
The autumn sky is a blue bowl cracked with thin clouds.
She lies on the ground and waits
for winter, for the full moon
to frost streets and signs and houses with its sexual light.
There below the broad-trunked oak we made love in glassy air,
your leather jacket creaking a little,
your tender hand beneath my neck,
roots digging their thumbs into my back,
mist of our breathing glowing under a moon-slicked
mandala of branches, shiver of limbs, map of intimate nerves.
She stands outside the building where once you lived,
cocks her head to read the titles of your books,
lies on the bed where you tied me with the gold cord of trust
as raindrops slapped fallen leaves.
She sails out across the window of rain,
its wind-spackled sea, shimmies
up a telephone pole, tightropes across its wires,
and surveys the highways we traveled to leave all this
and find ourselves here,
within driving distance from the end of the earth.

DIGRESSIONS

When I walk into this Minnesota truckstop,
and he slides his sweet ass across red vinyl
to sit beside me, I contemplate
how I might use him to settle the score
with you. Our baby busily rubs sugar
against the table's swirled Formica surface
and pulls open packages of grape jelly
and paints her face purple, as he tells me
I intrigue him. How about I fuck this trucker,
our daughter sleeping in the cab's front seat,
us moaning on the little bed in back.
Or maybe I'd say drive just drive and I'd
suck him and he would twist his wrist to rub
my clit and the semi's magic fingers
would vibrate us to rapture. Now he lets
me know he's got me pegged, some kind of artist,
some grown-up hippie-chick, who's got the done-
drugs glow. I guess the ghosts of Blake and Ginsberg
are peeking out my ears. I guess my past
bounds out to thwart my plain Midwest disguise.
He cannot know back then I tried to be
a man, to prove I could outdrink, outdose
myself with LSD, outfuck them all.
I made my anthem "Love the one you're with,"
all that optimistic victorious
reveling in the now, so I could make
my travel plans, so I could always be
two places at once. Listen, what if I
let my leg lean against his? What if I
let my finger outline his rose tattoo?
What if I wake up his forearm's skin?
I can see you fall into the abyss—

I kiss oblivion. Bye-bye, bye-bye.
Our girl's arranged florets of scrambled egg
and toast around the floor beneath her chair,
and I collect our things, tip big, and leave,
my headlights aiming downhill, down the dark
interstate—interstate—good word to name
digression—down the banks to black waters,
the Mississippi—I'm driving this road,
a common road my design was to avoid.
I hold you in me wherever I go,
and I, not you, am keeper of the faith.

GOOD FOR YOU

You sit in your holy chair among your holy books,
flipping through the pages of a magazine as I talk.
Good for you with your fingers in your blond hair,
for the azure in your eyes, the shoulders I love
to touch, sexy and broad in a sweatshirt,
your clever words. Good for you mesmerized
by music, making sentences. Good for you.
Good for you for being good in bed.
Good for everything I love about you hurting.
Good for you writing to your fiction writer friend:
"This other woman climbed inside my head
and implanted a picture of herself there.
She isn't a throw away fling sort of chick.
This is some hardcore woman. That makes me
a chump with a daughter and this whole
domestic set-up situation. Guess I'm a neophyte
to the cheatin' heart game." Good for the electric
shock under my fingernails, my heart short-circuiting.
Good for his advice: "If she hasn't left you yet, she won't—
she doesn't want to be stranded in South Dakota.
You must underplay the incident and lie.
You must make hollow promises. She will never
trust you again unless you reinvigorate lost love,
eat her pussy constantly, wait on her hand and foot
and prove your love. Question: Why did you confess?
Are you a stupid fucking asshole?" Glory be to men.
Glory be to cocks. Glory be to the altar on which
you, neophyte, sacrifice me. Raise your eyebrow,
and look toward me wasting away, your lies
parasites eating me from the inside out,
your promises hollowing out my cheeks and belly.
Give me an antibiotic. Give me a soporific.

HER FACE

I see her face in my mind's eye though I've never seen her face.
I hear her voice speaking to you of her home, the testimonials
of her life, the lives that went before, of her love for you
before she knew you. She knows your history, the small town
in Pennsylvania, the father who left, the mother who lay still
in sorrow, who kissed you between the eyes and opened
the eye inside, the blind grandfather who took you inside his mind
so you heard how to make light rainbow through the blinds,
how to make the smooth curve of the chair's arm gleam cherry,
how to make your words become clay, then to breathe movement
into your array of figurines. I see her face as surely as your story—
before you knew me, you woke to see your estranged lover making love
with another in the globe of your night mind. She called you forth
with the other inside her. I see her face for I have lain in bed
when we were apart and have spiraled out of my body to find you,
to touch the moon's face with my face, feel his cool cheek
shining light into your eyes. I have watched your closed eyes,
the quick little dance of the lids as you dream. I see her face
the way I used to see my own in you, my face in you called forth.

MS. KNIFE

She collects wedding rings,
          melts each gold *I love you*
down to her coin.

          She stands before my mirror
adorning herself with the power
          she gains by cutting between—jolt

of her steel shadow
          thrust against my ribs
as my husband and I make love—

          her eyes, blue lenses of surveillance,
blond hair, a veil of grief,
          her voice, the catchy tune of despair.

Her lips murmur, *never forget me,*
          never forget my kisses
or *my sibilant sighing name.*

          Her name is a knife
I sharpen daily to cut myself,
          to slice letters into my indelible skin.

She gives me the unspeakable:
          the tool to gouge open my scars
and make the nerves roar.

MY SWEET NOTHINGS

Do you taste me
       on his lips? Smell me
              on his skin? How good
I am when you kiss him
       and disclose our secrets.
              You feel the art
of my experienced hand, don't you?
       When your palm slides down his chest
              you learn the way to follow
the same slippery path
       he traces on my body, my length
              of thigh, curve of neck.
And do you lift my hairs from his sweater,
       to coil around your finger
              and slide up your sleeve?
Any part of me is a prized memento,
       for I am all over him, my musk
              in each of his pores, scent of our years.
Do you savor my voice
       in the quiet sighs between
              his words? How delicious I sound,
my cells caught between your teeth,
       my spice thrilling your taste buds.
              You've known me through him,
so tell me, my lover's lover—
       even now as this tart ink
              stains your tongue—
how much you like to take me in your mouth.

WILD WIND

I listen to the wind lecture across the northern plains
but it's not content. It rubs its shoulders
against the house—I guess it wants
to be understood, wants to slink
across the sky with lightning, that glamour queen,
wants to be one with it all, the sexy one, the warbler.
So it belts out a vibrato, then hardens itself,
yowling through storm windows, making the walls
of the house and the bed where I lie tremble.
And now it sobs. Why won't it stop
bellowing frustration? Calm down. Grow warm.
Settle into a murmur like our voices talking in the night,
though all the while, beyond will, I am wild for you.

SURGERY

The sunset surgeon makes a dire incision
into the chest of the sky, reveals organs
pulsing in the cavity of the self.
Soon night will come carrying an armful of stars,
that wide bandage, the Milky Way.
Where will I be in the darkness? Will I
see the shape of self as I lie blinking
at the bedroom blinds? Will I scrutinize
my anatomy? An organ for each emotion?
Will I hold a healing balm in my hand
or find the nurse who can take my pulse,
blood pressure, temperature, inject me
with the correct drugs—just enough poison
to kill my disease yet let the body fight back,
just enough pain killer to numb me yet let me
keep my eyes open, find a will.
Kiss my arms, these empty arms, my belly
hollowed out by woe. The skin of my thighs
misses yours. Kiss my head, my face,
this wanting place and each of my eyes
staring West at the stark hilless landscape.
Kiss my scars, the gash where I love you. Kiss me
wherever you can, wherever my soul might be.
Kiss me here, where it hurts

ONE DAY

"I thought we'd give it more time. . ." I said,
as I tried again to think in our quiet room.
I felt nothing save the sensation of photos,
us and our years, slipping silkily against my palms,
one by one. Our words lost syllables,
became a sound like leaves brushing leaves
as if we forgot what we were talking about.
I gave up words and lay down on the bed.
I don't know if I asked
you to come sit beside me or not.
You did. We agreed
we were sleepy yet touched throughout
the autumn afternoon. No illusion, no decision,
only daylight and peaceful sliding bodies.

LOVE ASLEEP

Tonight when you hold me in your sleep,
I know you love me again. Did you ever stop
or did I stop knowing or was your love asleep,
asleep as the body in pain, though morphine numbed,
rages against the brain's involuntary messages,
as the mind rages against the body for hurting,
against the union indivisible, the union cracked?
Was your love asleep as when the dreamer sees
emotions stand up incarnate with their painted faces,
boas, their enormous purple wings, sees them flash
their private parts from trenchcoats made of ink?
I guess you went to some inhospitable place
and I tried to follow. The dark comforted my eyes
yet I strained to see through the obscure blue,
to see the bright gash where you strode away
and streetlights cracked the night, glass shards
splintering out in circles. If I reached you, you shook
off my hand or turned your back or held my gaze
too briefly before you disappeared, leaving me
while your body stayed, terribly familiar.
So I lay down, my gut sliced down the center,
and babbled knowing I babbled,
making word sounds that were not words,
as I raved from half the split,
the mouth loosing syllables that craved meaning.
Tonight you hold me in your sleep. Yes. You hold me
in your sleep, your warm palm on my forehead.
Arms around torsos, legs across legs, our heated bodies
spiral around each other in sleep. Healing sleep,
reviving sleep, delicious sleep, sleep that cannot lie.

I TAKE THE STATEN ISLAND FERRY TO MEET YOU IN THE CITY

"Come here," she says in Texas drawl. "Come see."
Tourists lean against the rail of the Staten Island Ferry,
pull up their hoods against even this balmy November air,
       dance a cold dance on the deck.

She points quarter-activated binoculars at the Lady's torch and crown,
at the lights of Manhattan, skyscrapers rising from a core of night,
a diamond silently shooting stars and rainbows onto a shadowed wall.
       "Ya gotta see this."

"You assume and assume wrong," says man to boyfriend.
"Heard wrong. I didn't say that."
       I guess the water's hissing now.

I guess the water's lapping it up with its cat's tongue.
"Hurry up," says Texas. "I got a quarter for ya. Look! Focus."
       He complies, passionless, won't make her happy,

won't see the city in her eyes, won't feel her turned on
by the wind's rough skin on her face or the surge in her limbs

as she scales blazing towers. "Listen! This is not a postcard.
Not a photograph. You'll never see it like this."
       She spins toward him, then away,
       her red coat a cape that would tempt a bull

if there were one, if he weren't a roly-poly guy in a silly hunter's hat,
shuffling a little. "Okay," says boyfriend, "Okay."

And the two men look out toward Manhattan, forearms on the rail,
hands in prayer, muscular asses identically cocked.

The quarter moon glows between the Statue of Liberty
and the mirror-moon shaped arc of the Bayonne Bridge's blue lights.

Last time I saw you you said you were glad I came. Last time
you said I looked gorgeous in my coat. Midnight blue.
          I look good in night colors, I guess,

with taxis speeding down Houston and lit-up signs telling the truth,
how to be beautiful, be up-to-the minute stylish, stay healthy,
buy jewels as talismans for eternal love or dial 1-800-DIVORCE.
          Yeah, they make you want

to climb up to those slicked blow-job lips and straddle them
and fuck them until perfection and fucking be them.
          How will it be now, my love? After the crowds

rub against my midnight coat, after the city air blends in my blush
so you can't tell my healthy cheeks are make-believe.
          When you pull me to you on the street

where people and cars pass by fast, solid then ghost,
and when you kiss me as you have so many times in our marriage,
what will you see? Will you see diamonds everywhere?
          Streetlights, lighted windows, headlights,
          our eyes returning the light?

NOW WHAT?

Then while our baby and I napped
there came an awful thudding
as if the books all fell from the shelves
and our walls caved in,

as if the sky were falling
and everything in it—the stars and
satellites dropped from their orbits,
the planes from their flight paths,

as if birds' iced bodies hit the roof.
The sky is falling! My hen self squawked.
My chick cried out, "Who's that?"
(She didn't yet know when to say *what*.)

Americans Benumbed by Crisis,
read the headlines in my brain.
A Bitter House Debates.
President Impeached for Blow Jobs.

Market Confidence Volatile. The Day
You Nearly Left Me a Blizzard
Blasted So Hard it Shook the Bed.
Interstate Closed to Traffic. Goods Scarce.

Now what? I muttered
and followed the noise to my study.
Ancient plaster let loose from the lath
had crashed from the ceiling,

cracking the printer. I held our girl
in the ruins where heavy pieces littered

my desk and chair, saw I'd been spared.
I was not crushed in thought.

LOOKING BACK WITH THE ANGELS

Night comes early for the solstice is nearly here.
The sun hooks its orange chin on the shoulders of Nebraska,
then slips below the world and leaves embers and coals.
A squirrel—they're all fat now—runs high in the branches
of the elms and oaks and chestnuts that mesh over
the red sky. Our Christmas tree lights blink hypnotically
around the Indonesian angel, candy canes, wooden trains,
and polished papier-mâché apples. *All is calm, all is bright,*
I chant to myself as if the carols were piped in
from elsewhere, as if my inner space were an airport
or a department store. *Yeah, right,* I come back, remembering
our fights and the woman whom you once called a blessing.
In the dopey choir of my mind a hundred radio angels
lament cheating hearts. And there are angels everywhere,
in all the colored lights ringing trees and fences and houses,
in the nativity scenes, one whose wings span the tips
of the new moon and one looking over my shoulder,
whispering by turns good words, wishes of peace,
and curses, curses. *All is never-ending,* she says,
Words, acts can never be taken back. And she casts me
into the hell where the people's heads twist cruelly backward,
and they stride backward because deprived of forward vision,
where her face is your obsession—you hate me
and I hate my face in the mirror obscured by her blond light.
These days you say love me, your rapturous cock rising.
Right now you're upstairs with our daughter, giving her a bath.
I'm stuck in a painful torque, looking back. Be an angel,
untwist me and face me forward toward you. Guide me out.

ICON

You lay our daughter on the carpet
and tickled her and I laughed for joy,
for her joy and yours, for a pure moment
not suppressed by my sadness
as before when you threw her in the air,
and she looked at me to share her child glee
and I remembered to smile and why
I had to remember to smile,
to chant a nursery rhyme or play.
You and I and our child laughed together
and my thoughts were not
betrayals of the moment,
were not mirrors of your love withdrawn,
a face to face infinite regression
of reflections that even now are gone.

QUESTIONS ON SERIFOS

The half-moon lit gold
above the cupped hands of black mountains
is perfect.
I don't understand forgiveness.

Your snores mingle with our daughter's.
I watch headlights move up rock cliffs to the village,
motors groaning uphill,

people who have swum all day,
who ate by the sea, laughed, flirted, drank, danced.

No other women, I'll say, though we're both turned on.

People are so sexy here in Greece,
you feel giddy, cross and uncross your legs,
wiggle your foot just watching
the evening walkers move slowly in summer air,
the breeze teasing their skin with the taste of sea,
the lights of restaurants, bars, shops enticing.

What's your pleasure? A Greek salad, fresh bread,
ouzo, island-made wine, a silver bracelet of dolphins
to wear around your wrist as a talisman.

Sit down at this table, kick off your sandals,
let the sand sift through your toes, listen
to the *plash plash* of the Aegean on the shore.

No other women, you'll say, taking my hand,
squeezing it on my knee.

We've just made love
and I'm naked beneath your old denim shirt
which shrank too small for you.
Now you finger it when I wear it.

Such a beautiful shirt, you say, my old shirt.

What is forgiveness? Do I let go and forget?
Even now when it feels good,
feels good, feels good, my ghost slips out,
sits by my head, remembering her entering us.

I wish she would suffer as I did, and want you
to stand by, loving me as I kiss another.

The truth stinks when you tell it, sometimes,
just as the truth of our love smells
like the night-blooming jasmine, thyme,
and salt scents breathing into us,
invisible, intimate,
making our mouths water,
making us taste our bile and our hunger.

BEDTIME STORY ON SERIFOS

Tonight the moon rose over the island, full, orange, and laughing,
and made a wide orange path on the sea,
lighting *vous*, the deserted island called *ox*.

We carried our daughter through the village.
First I carried her, then you,
and I watched her watch

the children running through the square,
laughing and gathering around the ice cream chest
outside the fluorescent grocery store.

She lay her hand on one shoulder,
her cheek on the other
as you spoke to her and she to you.

I thought of the first time she said, "Moon,"
pointing to the light face
peeping through trees.

I didn't know then if you would be with us now
in the whitewashed village, this spiraling labyrinth
of the mountain, designed to confuse invading pirates.

We know our way here most of the time,
know the ten paths to our house,
which steps are most gradual,

the greetings to say to the old people who gather
to talk in the cool night and call out goodnight
and sweet dreams to passersby, while the owls call, too.

She cried, wouldn't let me put on her diaper
or pajamas, or kiss her or hold her,
wouldn't giggle when I tickled her.

You came from the shower, calmed her instantly
with your low voice, dressed her for bed,
read her to sleep.

She must have been tired from a day in the sea,
laughing in shallows. I worry her face
swollen from crying is a sign of unspoken sorrow.

You close the book when the lost invader,
tricked by the paths we walk each day,
turns away and fades into the sea's black periphery.

Good night, little girl. Good night, laughing moon.
She is safe now sleeping in your arms.
The village murmurs inscrutably with the owls' song

WALKING AROUND SANTA CRUZ

—Did I tell you I lived a while on Seabright Avenue?
And all night listened to the sea lions
making the dark go purple with their moans.
I was alone, nothing was familiar, no one was.
At daybreak I walked to the beach, carrying my shoes
in one hand, feeling the sidewalk bite the soles of my feet.
Sometimes the sky was blue, precise, almost shrill,
demanding I look at all the details: eaves of houses,
window moldings, texture of stucco, the succulents
whose names I didn't know, blooming in the beds,
the pampas grass's haughty plumes.
The ocean was macho, rough; waves reached
muscular fists high before breaking with a clap.

Santa Cruz was so beautiful I was bitter
about the beach parties and dance clubs and bars
and wondering whom I wanted, if I were wanted.
I was tired of men talking to me about astrology
or spirulina or James Joyce or Pablo Neruda,
then not delivering the goods. I was tired
of the tease—Stevie Wonder's Inner Visions
coiling heat around dancers swaying in sand,
all of us high on expertly bred sinsemilla,
and the music spiraling in the smoke of a bonfire
made from redwood that drifted down
the San Lorenzo River in winter storms.

A man taught me the names of the pepper tree
and cormorant and the lapis flowering bush,
ceanothus. See and know this
was my mnemonic. He said, "I love you."
Four days later he was gone.

He said, "I'm a seller of dreams."
Seems I spent hours a day wandering around,
conjuring up a friend I'd run into before it happened
just to test the squeaking doorhinges of clairvoyance.
—Could I enter there? Could I dream you into being?

A woman in orange told me of the New Age,
each tooth in her smile shone forth,
as if her face were a neon sign advertising promise.
I climbed the stairs of the St. George Hotel,
held the rail painted black, counted
my sandpaper steps against the wood as air rose,
a hard globe in my throat, the invisible world
of despair swelling. I made her
my hope. Her room stank of smoke.
She lay on a ratty futon. —Why are you here?
I looked at the books stacked against the walls,
at the walls a grimy color I couldn't name.

Outside I walked in the rain, past the bookstore,
the coffee roasting company, the Catalyst—the club
nicknamed the Cattle Lust where I met
a man and a woman who took me home
and tried to take me to bed. I was tired
of being a woman, of the venomous environment,
of umbrellas, of worrying—Is my bellybutton sexy?

The storms washed away West Cliff Drive,
washed away the restaurants and stores
on Capitola Beach, and I kept walking around
day and night, past the Coconut Grove Motel,
the surfers and tourists, down to the boardwalk
to listen to the roller coaster's clattering slats,
the screams I could hear from far away,
the moans of the sea lions I heard in my room

on Seabright Avenue—now that I've found you
and lost you and found you again, did I tell you?

Do you remember the early days, lying in bed,
telling each other postcards of our biographies?
I can see lights of the roller coaster
chasing each other in helixes, the ocean beyond,
pelicans swooping up supper from the waves,
the homeless under the bridges, stroking dogs.
I can see myself in yoga class hanging from rope
upside down. Maybe the blood in my head
would turn my third eye into matter,
so I could see the future and know to hang on
until you saw me and knew me.

My neighbor believed she could read the signs
in the woods, could watch the animals
and predict the date of the Big One, the quake
that would crack the holy cross into smithereens—
Mother Earth having multiple orgasms, she said.
When she was wrong, she lit some candles
in the corners of her house, burned some sage,
closed her eyes and fists, opened them
and found new numbers inscribed in her palm.
I closed my eyes and found nothing in my hands,
only my yearning, only my long lifeline.

NOTES

The epigraph of Part 1 is from the poem "How Would It be?" by Gerald Stern.

Rainy Ghazal. "Rain down rain down rain down rain down" is taken from a concrete poem by Mary Ellen Solt.

Cavafy's Ghost Visits Me at my Mailbox at Bucknell University. The lines of the epigraph are from Constantine Cavafy's poem, "The God Abandons Antony," translated by Aliki Barnstone and Willis Barnstone.

The epigraphs of Part 2 and Part 3 by Saint John and Sappho are translated by Willis Barnstone.

Wild With It. The epigraph is from Whitman's "Song of Myself."

Digressions. Thanks to Tony Hoagland for the conversation that sparked this poem.

With Walt Whitman on the Staten Island Ferry. The epigraph is from Whitman's "Crossing Brooklyn Ferry."

Looking Back with the Angels contains lines derived from Robert Pinsky's translation of Canto XX of Dante's Inferno.

Walking Around Santa Cruz. The title and some lines are derived from Pablo Neruda's poem, "Walking Around."

AUTHOR BIO

Aliki Barnstone is a poet, translator, and scholar, whose books of poems include *The Real Tin Flower* (introduced by Anne Sexton), *Windows in Providence*, and most recently, *Madly In Love*. She is the editor of *Voices of Light: Spiritual and Visionary Poems by Women around the World from Ancient Sumeria to Now*. Her poems have appeared in *Agni, Boulevard, The New England Review, New Letters, The Southern Review, The Southwest Review, TriQuarterly,* and elsewhere. She is Professor at the University of Nevada, Las Vegas.